Baby Oh Baby - A Record of Baby's First Year

Illustration Copyright © 2000 Debbie Mumm
www.debbiemumm.com

Text Copyright © 2000
The Brownlow Corporation
6309 Airport Freeway
Fort Worth, Texas 76117

Designed by Koechel Peterson & Associates

ISBN 1-57051-486-0

Printed in USA

BABY OH BABY

A RECORD OF BABY'S FIRST YEAR

Illustrated by

DEBBIE MUMM®

BABY DEAR

Where did you come from, baby dear?
"Out of the everywhere into here."

Where did you get those eyes so blue?
"Out of the sky as I came through."

What makes the light in them sparkle and spin?
"Some of the starry spikes left in."

Where did you get that little tear?
"I found it waiting when I got here."

What makes your forehead so smooth and high?
"A soft hand stroked it as I went by."

What makes your cheek like a warm soft rose?
"I saw something better than anyone knows."

Whence that three-cornered smile of bliss?
"Three angels gave me at once a kiss."

Were did you get this precious ear?
"God spoke and it came out to hear."

Where did you get those arms and hands?
"Love made itself into bonds and bands."

Feet, whence did you come, you darling things?
"From the same box as cherubs wings."

How did they all just come to be you?
"God thought about me and so I grew."

But how did you come to us, you dear?
"God thought about you, and so I am here."

GEORGE MACDONALD

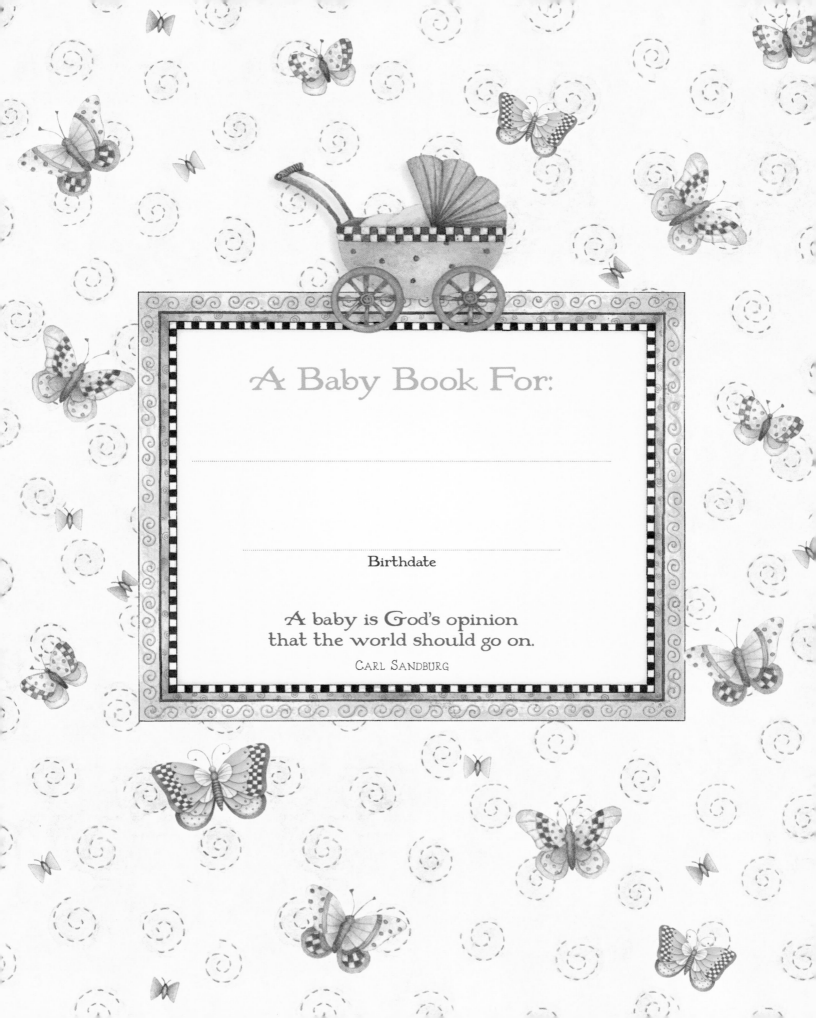

A Baby Book For:

....

....

Birthdate

A baby is God's opinion
that the world should go on.

CARL SANDBURG

The Wonderful News!

When I found out that you were on the way

My due date

My reaction was

How I told your father

His reaction was

We celebrated by

The first people we told were

Their reactions were

Special Moments

The first time I heard your heartbeat

Mom's cravings

Nicknames before you were born

The first time you moved

The first time I saw you . . .

-Place sonogram here-

Date

Number of weeks

Preparing for You

My Doctor ....

Special Instructions ....

....

....

How I felt about being pregnant ....

....

....

My age when you were born .... Your father's age when you were born ....

Helpful books we read ....

....

....

Advice from family and friends ....

....

....

....

....

Mom's Progress

PHOTO OF MOM AT 3 MONTHS

PHOTO OF MOM AT 6 MONTHS

PHOTO OF MOM AT 8 ½ MONTHS

You saw me before I was born...
PSALM 139:16

A letter from Dad

Nothing creates a firmer belief in heredity
than having a beautiful baby.

A letter from Mom

A baby is born with the need to be loved
and never outgrows it.

You received	From

Children
are a gift
from God.
PSALM 127:3

You received   From

You're Here!

You arrived at (time) .... • On (date) ....

At (place) ....

A little about my labor ....

....

Who was there

....

....

....

....

The first thing I said when you were born ....

....

The first thing your father said when you were born ....

....

....

Babies are like sponges. They absorb all your strength and
leave you limp. But give them a squeeze and you get it all back.

Birth Announcement

PLACE BIRTH ANNOUNCEMENT HERE

Your weight .... Your length ....

The color of your eyes .... The color of your hair ....

Your distinguishing characteristics ....

....

....

Babies are such a nice way to start people.

About Your Name

Your Name

Its meaning

How it was chosen

Other names we considered

Your nicknames

Your First Photo

PLACE PHOTO HERE

A babe is nothing but a bundle of possibilities. HENRY WARD BEECHER

Your little handprint

Your little footprint

Birth Certificate

PLACE BIRTH
CERTIFICATE HERE

Hospital Bracelet

PLACE HOSPITAL BRACELET HERE

You Finally Came Home

Date .... Time ....

Where we lived ....

....

You wore ....

....

The weather was ....

....

Your reaction to the outside world ....

....

....

Your Nursery was decorated ....

....

....

....

A babe in the house is a well-spring of pleasures,
a messenger of peace and love, a resting place for innocence on earth,
a link between angels and men.
MARTIN F. TUPPER

The World Around You

Current news events ....

....

....

....

President of the U.S. ....

Best selling books

....

....

Popular sports figures

....

....

....

Popular musical groups

....

....

....

♪♫ Popular songs ♪♫

....

....

Popular movies

....

....

....

Popular TV Shows

....

....

....

Popular movie stars

....

....

....

a gallon of milk $ ....

a postage stamp $ ....

a movie ticket $ ....

a gallon of gas $ ....

Your Family

Mother

Father

Birth date

Birth date

Birth place

Birth place

Your brothers and sisters

Name

Name

Birth date

Birth date

Birth place

Birth place

Name

Birth date

Birth place

Name

Birth date

Birth place

Name

Birth date

Birth place

Name

Birth date

Birth place

FEATHERED NEST

· ROCK·a·bye BABIES ·

Your Family History

Maternal Grandmother	Paternal Grandmother

Maternal Grandfather	Paternal Grandfather

Maternal Great-grandmother	Paternal Great-grandmother

Maternal Great-grandfather	Paternal Great-grandfather

Maternal Great-grandmother	Paternal Great-grandmother

Maternal Great-grandfather	Paternal Great-grandfather

Our children are living messages we send to a time and place we will not see.

Mom's Story

My name is

_____

I grew up

_____

_____

My brothers and sisters

_____

_____

I attended school at

_____

_____

My talents and hobbies are

_____

_____

I met your father

He grew up

His brothers and sisters

He attended school at

We dated for

We were married on (date)

At (place)

First Visitors

Name   What they said about you

_____   _____

_____   _____

_____   _____

_____   _____

_____   _____

_____   _____

Who they thought you looked like

_____

_____

_____

Your First Days at Home

Your sleeping habits _____

_____

_____

Your eating habits _____

_____

_____

Who helped take care of you

_____   _____

_____   _____

_____   _____

Moments we'll never forget _____

Home Sweet Home _____

_____

_____

People who say they sleep like a baby usually don't have one.
LEO J. BURKE

You Grew So Fast!

Date	Age	Height	Weight

Medical Information

Your Pediatrician ....

	Date	Type
Vaccinations	....	....
	....	....
	....	....
	....	....
	....	....
	....	....
	....	....

First Tooth .... Second Tooth ....

Third Tooth .... Fourth Tooth ....

Others ....

....

Famous Firsts

Slept through the night

Ate solid food

Rolled over

Clapped

Discovered your hands

Tooth

Discovered your feet

Said "Mama"

Held a bottle

Said "Dada"

Crawled

Stood

Played with a toy

Took a step

Waved bye~bye

Give a little love to a child, and you get a great deal back.
JOHN RUSKIN

Your First Journey

Date .... Destination ....

Memorable moments ....

....

....

....

....

Your First Haircut

Date .... By Whom ....

Before photo

LOCK OF
HAIR HERE

After photo

It's Bedtime

Where you slept ....

How you slept ....

How we put you back to sleep after you woke ....

....

When you first slept through the night ....

Your nap schedule ....

....

When you moved from crib to bed ....

....

....

How we decorated your bedroom ....

....

....

Now I lay me down to sleep.

I pray Thee, Lord, my soul to keep;

Thy love stay with me through the night

And wake me with the morning light.

Your favorite bedtime stories

....

....

Your favorite lullaby ....

Who put you to bed ....

Your favorite sleep toy ....

Your favorite pajamas ....

Your favorite blanket ....

Your Special Day

Special Service

Date .... Time ....

Place

The service was conducted by

You wore

Guests	Gifts

PHOTO PAGE

Every baby comes with the message
that God is not yet discouraged.
RABINDRANATH TAGORE

Your First Christmas

Christmas Eve ....

....

We celebrated Christmas at ....

....

We shared the season with ....

....

....

....

Gifts you received

....

....

....

....

Your reactions to your first Christmas ....

....

NOEL

Fa La La La La La La La La

CHRISTMAS PHOTOS

And the angel said to them,
"Behold, I bring you glad tidings
of great joy."

LUKE 2:10

Your First Easter

We spent Easter at ....

....

We celebrated with ....

....

....

Your Easter outfit ....

....

Your First Thanksgiving

We spent Thanksgiving at

We celebrated with

What we were most thankful for

PLACE PHOTO HERE

Other Holidays

Special Events

There are 152 distinctly different ways
of holding a baby—and all of them are right.

HEYWOOD BROUN

A Few of Your Favorite Things

Stuffed Toy

Bedtime Story

Play Toy

Book

Bath Toy

Food

Lullaby

Playmate

Blanket

People

Others

Your First Outings

First trip to visit relatives

Where we took walks

Your favorite parks and playgrounds

Your first day trips

How you responded to being in a car

Your favorite outdoor activity

Your first night away from home

Fun weekend activities

Memorable Moments of Your First Twelve Months

First Month

Second Month

Third Month

Fourth Month

Fifth Month

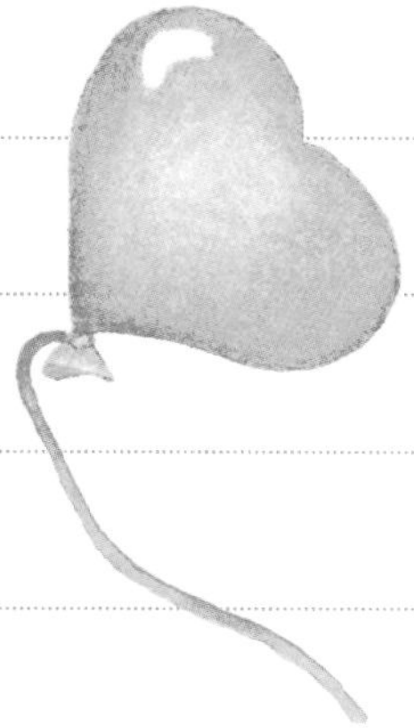

Sixth Month

Seventh Month

Eighth Month

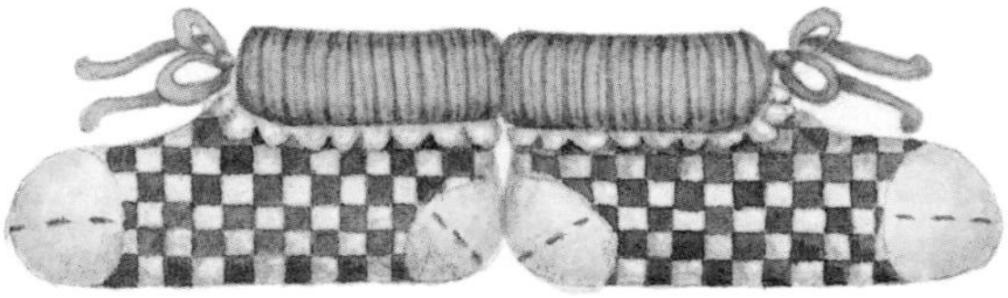

Ninth Month

Tenth Month

Eleventh Month

Twelfth Month

Do everything, even the little things, in love.
1 CORINTHIANS 16:14

1 year old

How we celebrated

Friends and family that shared the occasion

Place photo here

Gifts

PHOTOS

A child reaches for your hand
and touches your heart.

2 years old

How we celebrated

Friends and family that shared the occasion

Gifts

Place photo here

Birthday Greetings

3 years old

How we celebrated

Friends and family that shared the occasion

Gifts

Place photo here

BEST WISHES ON YOUR BIRTHDAY

4 years old

How we celebrated

Friends and family that shared the occasion

Gifts

Place photo here

Happy Birthday to you

5 years old

How we celebrated

Friends and family that shared the occasion

Gifts

Place photo here

We must view children not
as empty bottles to be filled,
but as candles to be lit.

ROBERT H. SHAFFER

6 Sixth

7 Seventh

IT'S A PARTY!

8 Eighth

9 Ninth

10 Tenth

PHOTOS

Your First Masterpieces

I love little children, and it is not a slight thing when they,
who are fresh from God, love us.

CHARLES DICKENS

Favorite Photos

Favorite Photos

Children are the hands by
which we take hold of heaven.

A Hundred Years From Now

...it will not matter
what my bank account was,
the sort of house I lived in,
or the kind of car I drove.
But the world may be different
because I was important
in the life of a child.